Commercial Manufacturing Company

A Brief History of the Mege Discovery

Oleomargarine Butter or Butterine

Commercial Manufacturing Company

A Brief History of the Mege Discovery
Oleomargarine Butter or Butterine

ISBN/EAN: 9783337128951

Printed in Europe, USA, Canada, Australia, Japan

Cover: Foto ©Andreas Hilbeck / pixelio.de

More available books at **www.hansebooks.com**

A BRIEF HISTORY

OF THE

MÉGE DISCOVERY.

Oleomargarine Butter

OR

BUTTERINE.

MICROSCOPICALLY AND CHEMICALLY ANALYZED BY THE MOST SKILLFUL
AND DISTINGUISHED SCIENTISTS,

DEMONSTRATING ITS PURITY.

Award of the AMERICAN INSTITUTE, *and Opinions of* PROF. C. F. CHANDLER, *President of
the New York Board of Health;* PROF. GEORGE F. BARKER, *of the University of Pennsylvania;* DR. HENRY A. MOTT, JR., *of New York;* PROF. S. C. CALDWELL, *of Cornell University;* PROF. S. W. JOHNSON, *of Yale College;* PROF. C. A. GOESSMANN, *of
the Massachusetts Agricultural College;* PROF. HENRY MORTON, *of the Stevens
Institute of Technology, of Hoboken;* DR. CHARLES P. WILLIAMS, *of
Philadelphia;* PROF. ATWATER, *of the Wesleyan University,
and* PROF. ARNOLD, *of the University of New York.*

NEW YORK:

Commercial Manufacturing Company Consolidated,
48TH STREET AND NORTH RIVER.
1881.

Oleomargarine Butter

OR

BUTTERINE.

BEFORE the Social Science Association, convened at Saratoga in the summer of 1879, Mr. George T. Angell of Boston, President of the Society for the Prevention of Cruelty to Animals, delivered an address on the Adulteration of Food. He dwelt at length on the impurity of oleomargarine butter (butterine), and made a series of most unjust and unfounded statements against its wholesomeness. This, from a man who does not even pretend to be a scientific man, and who never made a chemical analysis in his life, was a pretty bold undertaking. The only groundwork he had for the statements he made were taken from an article of one John Michell, an amateur microscopist having no scientific standing and whose labor in every field, even to the examination of a drop of water, is the subject of scientific ridicule, and who sold the result of his sensational article on oleomargarine to a dairy paper for twenty-five dollars. It is the object of this pamphlet to present a full and minute examination of the whole subject of oleomargarine, briefly considering the result of the investigation of the leading scientific men in this country.

The American Chemist, a monthly journal edited by
Prof. C. F. Chandler, Professor of Chemistry at Colum-
bia College, New York, and by other eminent scientific
men, published in April of 1874, an extract from a
report made by M. Felix Baudet, to the Board of
Health of the Department of the Seine, on the product
presented under the name of artificial butter by M. Mége
Mauries. It was translated from the *Moniteur Scien-
tifique* by Fred. A. Hoadley, B. A., and is as follows:

Some years ago, at a time when M. Mége Mauries,
commissioned by the government to investigate several
questions of domestic economy, was busy improving the
ordinary manufacture of bread, he was invited to make
some researches with a view to obtain, for the use of
the navy and of the poorer classes, a product suitable
to take the place of ordinary butter, to be sold at a much
less price, and capable of being kept without becoming
rancid, as butter does in a little while. M. Mége under-
took for this purpose the following

EXPERIMENTS AT THE FARM AT VINCENNES:

He placed several milch cows on a strict diet; soon
these cows experienced a decrease in weight, and furnished a proportionately less amount of milk, but this
milk always contained butter. Where could the butter
come from? M. Mége believed that it was produced
from the fat of the animal, which, being absorbed and
carried into the circulation, was deprived of its stearine
by respiratory combustion, and furnished its oleomarga-

rine to the udders, where, under the influence of the mammary pepsin, it was changed into butyric oleomargarine; that is to say, into butter. Guided by this information, M. Mége attempted immediately to copy the natural operation, by using at first cow's fat, then beef suet; and he was not long in obtaining, by a process as simple as it is ingenious, a fat fusible, at nearly the same temperature as butter, of a sweet and agreeable taste. He then succeeded in transforming this same fat into butter, by a process similar to that of nature. Starting from the well-known fact that fats are changed in the presence of animal substances, and with a rapidity so much the greater according as they are the longer in contact with them, and according as the temperature is the more elevated, he endeavored first to melt some beef fat at a temperature of only forty-five or fifty degrees; he obtained in this way a product without taste and free from foreign odor, which afforded an excellent base for the preparation of butter. He accomplished this as follows:

"THE FAT OF NEWLY SLAUGHTERED BEEF

of the best quality was ground up between two cylinders, whose conical teeth crushed it and tore open the membranes which enveloped it. After having undergone this grinding, it fell into a deep vat heated by steam, and into which there was turned for every thousand kilogrammes of fat three hundred kilogrammes of water. The temperature of the mixture was then carried to 45° centigrade, and the mass was carefully stirred. At the end of two hours the fat separated from the membranes which enveloped it. By means of a flexible tube, tipped with the knob of a sprinkling pot, it is then led off into a second vat, heated by a water-bath to thirty or forty degrees, when there is added two per cent. of sea salt, in order to facilitate the depuration. In two hours this fat is separated from the fragments of animal substances which have escaped the dissolving action of the pepsin, and from the water which it still retains; it becomes clear and presents a beautiful yellow color, and an odor very similar to that of butter newly churned. It may now be solidified in tin coolers of from twenty-five to thirty liters capacity. These coolers, as soon as they are filled, are placed in a room maintained at a temperature of twenty or twenty-five degrees, where they are slowly cooled. The following day the fat, having acquired a semi-solid consistence, presents a granulated appearance, as if crystallized, which renders it very suitable for subjection to the action of a press. It is then cut into cakes, packed in linen and placed under a hydraulic press. Under the influence of careful pressure, in a room maintained at a temperature of about twenty-five degrees, this fat is separated into two very nearly equal parts; one, which represents forty or fifty per cent. of the material, is the stearine. fusible between fifty and fifty-nine degrees, which remains in the linen; the other is the liquid oleomargarine, in amount equal to five or six tenths of the fat upon which we operated. The stearine is employed in the manufacture of candles; it may be used to make stearine candles or stearine acid candles. As for the oleomargarine, when it has been congealed by cooling, it presents a granulated appearance, a color slightly yellow, and an agreeable taste. Besides, it melts perfectly in the mouth, like butter, while beef fat, under the same condition, is separated into oleomargarine, which dissolues into stearine, which adheres more or less to the palate. The oleo-margarine thus obtained, passed through cylinders

UNDER A SHOWER OF WATER,

in order to wash it and give to it a homogeneous con-sistence, constitutes an excellent cooking substance. and is intended to replace, with advantage and with economy, the different fats, and even butter, in ordinary cooking. It is especially valuable for the navy on ac-count of the facility with which it may be preserved a very long time without becoming rancid. It is actually sold in Paris under the name of margarine, at from eighty centimes to a franc for half a kilogramme. It is already very much in demand. It is with oleomarga-rine that M. Mége. by operating in the following manner, makes his butter: Having observed that the mammary glands of the cow, which secrete the milk, contain a peculiar substance, a kind of pepsin, endowed with the power of emulsionizing fat with water, he used this observation to transform the oleomargarine into cream, and finally this cream into butter. He placed in a churn fifty kilogrammes of oleomargarine melted, about twenty-five liters of cow's milk, which represent less than one kilogramme of butter, and twenty-five kil-ogrammes of water containing the soluble parts of 100 grains of the mammary glands of the cow, very finely divided and kept for some time in maceration. He adds a small quantity of annotto, in order to give the color. The churn is then set in motion, and at the end of a quarter of an hour the oleo and the water become emulsionized and transformed into a thick cream, simi-

lar to that of milk. By continuing the motion of the
churn the cream changes in its turn into butter, in a
longer or shorter time, according to the conditions of
the operation—usually two hours suffice. The churning being ended, some cold water is poured into the
churn, and the butter separates, containing, like ordinary
butter, buttermilk. The product is then placed in an
apparatus like a kneading machine, and composed of
two cylindrical crushers placed under a stream of water.
There it is worked in a way to change it into well-
washed butter, of fine and homogeneous consistence.
This butter, washed with water at the ordinary temperature, contains, according to my experiments performed
with L. Hote in the laboratory of M. Peligot, 12.5 per
cent. of water, leaving a residue when dissolved in ether
weighing 1.20 for every hundred grammes in the dry
state, and of two specimens, one solidified. I mean by
solidification point the thermometric degrees observed
at the moment when the instrument,

PLUNGED INTO THE LIQUID BUTTER,

ceases for an instant to fall, at the same time the butter commences to become solid, and rises soon by the
influence of the heat generated by the solidification at
twenty-two degrees, the other at seventeen degrees,
while beef fat becomes solid between thirty-two and
thirty-three degrees. For the fine merchantable butter
of Paris I have found nineteen degrees as the point of
solidification. On the other hand, I have found 22.2
degrees for the ordinary butter of Calvado. According
to the experiments of M. Bouissingault in butter carefully prepared, well washed and dried, the proportion

of water is from thirteen to fourteen per cent. It increases to eighteen and to twenty and twenty-four per cent. in the market butter of ordinary and inferior quality. I have found 11.94 per cent. in the butter of Isigny and 13.38 per cent. in the ordinary butter of the Calvados.

"In regard to the caseous matter insoluble in the ether, the butter of Isigny, first quality, gave me 3.13 grammes in 100 grammes of the dry substance, while I have obtained only 1.20 grammes in 100 of the dry residue with the butter of M. Mége. This artificial butter presents, then, this advantage, that it contains much less water and animal substance, which makes the ordinary commercial butter rancid; moreover, for the same weight, it furnishes more genuine butter. The two circumstances assist, without doubt, in its preservation, which is much more perfect than that of common butter. They also prevent it from acquiring the odor and the acridity which are soon developed in the latter. During warm weather, when ordinary butter can with difficulty be preserved from melting, it is easy to give to the artificial butter a more or less solid consistence by preparing an oleomargarine more or less free from stearine. On the other hand, M. Mége has observed that by washing his butter with water at a temperature of only five or six degrees, he is able to leave in it less water, and thus to obtain a product capable of being kept a very long time. A specimen of butter thus prepared, and which M. Mége called 'butter without water,' carried from Paris to Vienna, in Austria, the 29th of October, 1871, has just been brought back, on the 5th of April, and is found still, after five months,

IN A GOOD STATE OF PRESERVATION.

" In order to fully appreciate the value of the product of M. Mege as regards domestic economy and hygiene, I have requested several of my colleagues to try the oleomargarine and the artificial butter; I have submitted this product to the judgment of several breeders and butter merchants of the Auge valley; I have used it myself also in my household, and we have all been of the opinion that the oleomargarine constitutes an excellent butter for the kitchen, and that if the artificial butter has not the fine and aromatic taste of the Normandy butter for eating with bread, or use in culinary preparations, it does afford, in many other respects, the qualities of ordinary butter perfectly. The experiments which I have witnessed in the works of M. Mége, those which I have myself made, or which have been made at my instance on the new products which he has brought forward, authorize me to believe that he has realized a happy application of his knowledge and his inventive genius in this employment of beef fat, and that he has furnished for consumption two new and important products. The first, called oleomargarine, offers a valuable material for cooking purposes, especially for naval vessels during long voyages, by reason of its good quality, and of its capability of long and excellent preservation. The second, possessed of properties which allow of its close comparison with butter in a chemical point of view, as well as regards its uses, may take the place of the latter in many instances; and in consequence of the small expense at which it can be made, it has been put in competition with milk butter, which will lower necessarily the price of the latter, to

the benefit of the consumer, which will render the consumption of it less considerable, and will allow the
breeders to devote a greater quantity of milk to the
raising of calves, a great advantage to this industry.

"As regards healthfulness, it is evident that the
origin and preparation of these two products presented
by M. Mége do not afford any circumstance which can
render their consumption a matter of suspicion. There
is, then, no reason for opposing the sale of these products,
if we include the proviso that that which M. Mége Mauries compares to butter is not really butter in the usual
and true acceptation of the word. It should not be sold
under the name of butter, but under a particular desig-
nation, which will permit it to be distinguished from
butter properly so called, or milk butter."

THE AUTHORITY ABOVE QUOTED,

in a chemical and scientific point of view, bearing on any
ordinary subject, would not be questioned, but would be
sufficient to convince any candid and intelligent mind
that there cannot be a shadow of doubt as to the importance of this discovery and the great benefits derived
therefrom by furnishing to the people a healthful article
of diet.

Yet when we consider that this new product is put
forward as a substitute for butter, an article which
enters into the daily consumption of every family in this
and other civilized countries, it is evident that a matter
of such vast importance is worthy of careful investigation. "The *Encyclopedia Britannica*,* the highest au-

* Johnson's Encyclopedia, Vol. 1, p. 685; American Encyclopedia, Vol.
12, p. 614.

thority known, treats of oleomargarine butter (butterine, as it is known in Europe) as follows, in volume four, under the title of ' Butter.' "

" Under the name of butterine, an artificial substitute for butter has been introduced in America and imported into England from New York. It is the same as the artificial butter, or ' *margarine-mauries*,' which has been for some years manufactured in Paris according to a method made public by the eminent chemist, M. Mége Mauries. Having surmised that the formation of butter contained in milk was due to the absorbtion of fat contained in the animal tissues, M. Mauries was led to experiment upon the splitting up of animal fat. The process he ultimately adopted consisted in heating finely minced beef suet with water. The mixture he raised to a temperature of 45° C. (113° Fahr.) He removed the fatty matter and submitted it, when cool, to powerful hydraulic pressure, separating it into stearine and oleomargarine, which last alone he used for butter-making. Of this oil, about the proportion of ten pounds, with four pints of milk and three pints of water, were placed in a churn, to which a small quantity of annotto was added for coloring, and the whole churned together. The product so obtained, when well washed, was, in general appearance, taste, and consistency, like ordinary butter, and when well freed from water, it was found to keep a longer time. According to French official reports, artificial butter goes much farther as food than the genuine article, and forms a perfectly wholesome *dietic* material. The Parisian octroi officials have recognized the efficiency of the substitute by imposing on it the same duties which are chargeable on ordinary butter. The company was established, and the manufacture in France had in 1874, seven manufactories, in which 400 men were employed." There can be no doubt that the product obtained by the process of M. Mége Mauries is a safe and more wholesome article than the unsavory, rancid butter which is sold so extensively. We find this industry was practically established, and its product introduced into commerce in the large cities of the East, where the demand and consumption of oleomargarine butter grew so rapidly that much capital was applied to its manufacture, by the erection of large factories, on such an expensive scale that the great mass of butter made by the old dairy system was forced out of the market, at a heavy loss to the producer and commission merchant who had made his advances. This led to the organization of a society composed of farmers and commission men, who enlisted in one common cause, banded together, raised subscriptions to employ private policemen and detectives, and adopted every unfair means to injure and destroy the manufacture of this product. Falsehoods the most malignant were industriously circulated; prejudices were played upon, and artful and unconstitutional laws were passed, to assist them in their attempts to crush a rival so formidable to the old method of producing butter. Laws were passed to suit their purposes, not to protect the interests of the people. Special acts were passed in nearly all the States where the industry had been established; yet, in the face of all legislation and misrepresentation, oleomargarine grew rapidly into favor.

THIS CONTINUAL AND BITTER OPPOSITION

led the thinking portion of the public to investigate

for themselves, whereupon the superiority of oleomargarine to a large proportion of dairy butter was proved. As a last resort the organization called to their assistance one John Michell, a so-called microscopist, who claimed to discover that the product contained numbers of living objects. These assertions were published broadcast, with a view to alarm unthinking people. This vicious misrepresentation was taken up by the manufacturers of oleomargarine butter; and for the purpose of exposing the false statements made by Michell, had their several products critically examined under the microscope, and compared with dairy butter, by the highest authority in this country in that branch of science, Prof. J. W. S. Arnold, of the University Medical College of New York, and the result was published in a letter from Dr. Mott in the *New York Times*, from which the following is taken:

"OLEOMARGARINE BUTTER—RECENT MICROSCOPIC TESTS.

" PROF. MOTT'S REPLY TO JOHN MICHELL—COMPARATIVE PURITY OF DAIRY BUTTER AND THE ARTICLE OF COMMERCE.

" Prof. Mott has recently made microscopic tests of samples of dairy butter and oleomargarine butter. The result of his labors will be found in the subjoined communication. He shows a grade of purity in the new article of commerce, and in what particulars it equals certain grades of dairy butter.

" *To the Editor of the New York Times*—In a recent number of a dairy organ there appeared an article on oleomargarine, by one John Michell, the object of which was evidently an attempt to damage the oleomargarine industry. The writer presents two microscopical plates illustrating oleomargarine butter and natural butter as they appear under the microscope to him. I hardly know how to express myself with respect to Mr. Michell, but one thing is certain, that this plate representing oleomargarine butter was either intentionally originated to create a sensation, or that Mr. Michell himself is a person perfectly incompetent to make microscopical investigations. This, I think, will be clearly demonstrated to any fair-minded man farther on in this paper. Mr. Michell states in his article that the close resemblance of oleomargarine to butter suggested to him the propriety of making a microscopical examination of both substances, to see if they could be distinguished by such means. This suggestion was a good one, and, had he carried it out conscientiously, science would be at least benefited by examination. Seeing the importance of a thorough microscopical investigation after such gross misrepresentations as have been presented by Mr. Michell, I visited Prof. J. W. S. Arnold, Professor of Histology and Microscopy in the University Medical College of this city, who is acknowledged to be one of the leading microscopists in this country, and engaged him to make the investigation. Not being satisfied with a microscopical examination of the butter alone, I determined to have examined caul-fat, stearine, oleomargarine (before being churned), and oleomargarine butter, and compare the same with natural butter, both pure and rancid. The samples examined by Prof. Arnold were obtained from the Commercial Manufacturing Company, by myself in person, and given to him.

"Figure 1 represents caul-fat under the microscope, the crystalline nature and adipose tissue being clearly seen, as also a globule of oil.

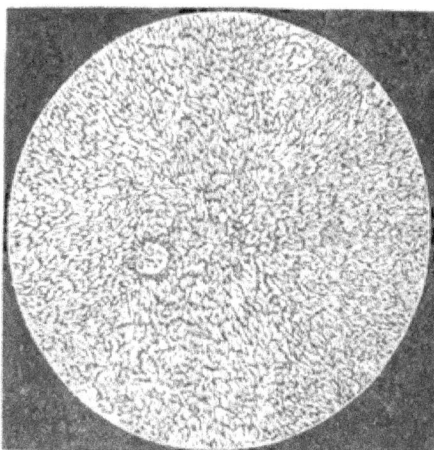

Fig. 1.

"Figure 2 represents oleomargarine before it is churned, or what is known as oleomargarine oil. It

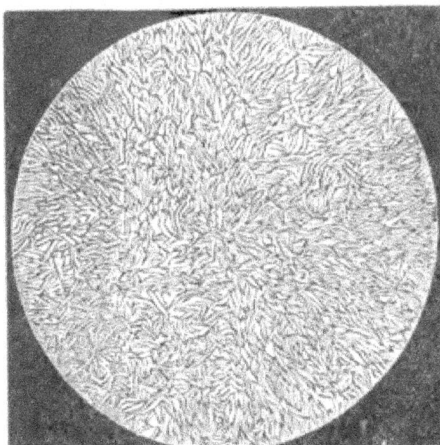

Fig. 2.

will be seen from this plate that oleomargarine before being churned is entirely in a crystalline condition.

" It will be necessary, before proceeding to a description of the other plate, to explain the cause of crystallization. The crystalline condition of oleomargarine oil is due to the fact that the oil is allowed to cool gradually, and then crystallized to a solid condition. To demonstrate this point most emphatically to your readers, I directed Prof. Arnold to melt a sample of natural butter, allow the same to cool slowly to a solid condition, and then make a microscopical examination, the result of which is illustrated in Figure 3.

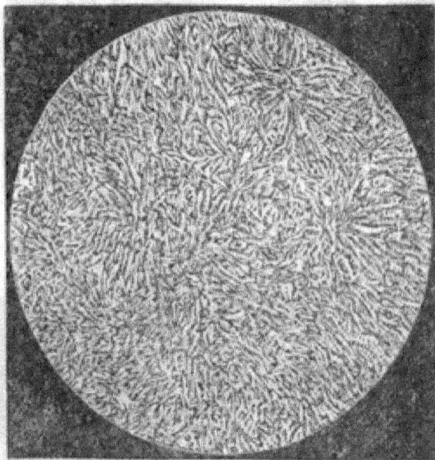

Fig. 3.

" From this figure it will at once be seen that the mass is entirely crystallized, and in no way differs from oleomargarine oil, as shown in Figure 2.

" Figure 4 represents oleomargarine butter, and Figure 5 natural butter. It will be seen by examination of these two figures that they consist of an innumerable number of minute globules of varying size, but not a trace of a crystal appears in either; nor is there seen any contorted shape, imaginary figures or bodies, as

2

represented in Figure 6, which is Michell's representation of oleomargarine butter.

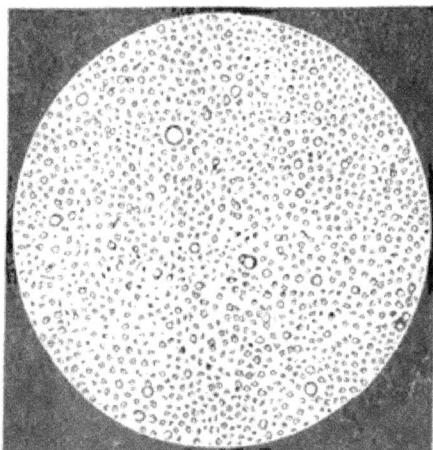

Fig. 4.

" I quote the following paragraph from an article published by Michell on the 'Microscope and its Misrep-

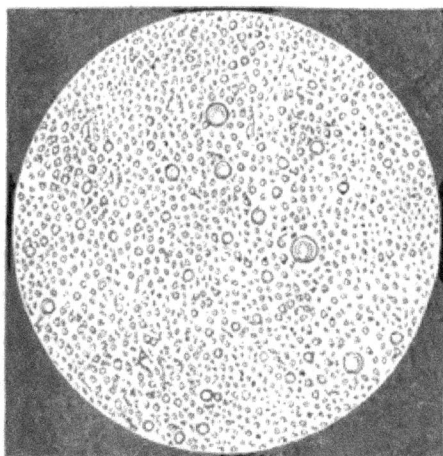

Fig. 5.

resentations': 'The fact that most skillful microscopists of the age all differ upon the true appearance of a

common and not very minute object, and the microscope itself presenting to the vision the most opposite
appearances of one and the same object, should act as
a caution to those who accept too readily theories
based upon microscopical researches.' If this remarkable and spontaneous effusion is true about skillful
microscopists, how much more important it is to receive with the very greatest caution the inaccurate or
manufactured results of an amateur microscopist! The

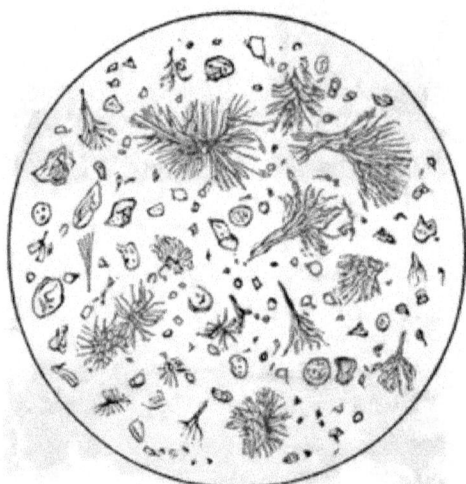

Fig. 6.

remarkable illustration by Michell, shown in Figure 6,
when compared with the accurate illustration by Prof.
Arnold, shows at once that the former was obtained
by a person perfectly incompetent to make a microscopical examination. If Michell did obtain under the
microscope any such illustration as shown in Figure 6,
it only demonstrates more clearly how incompetent he
is to make the examination; for the contorted-shaped
bodies can only be explained (if at all) by the glass
cover pressing too hard on the butter under examina-

tion. The crystals of fat which are represented are seldom present in *freshly made oleomargarine or natural butter*, but sometimes form after either butter has been kept for some time. If the butter softens, crystals of fat are formed when it solidifies again, in both cases.

"In the editorial notice on Mr. Michell's article I find the following: 'The writer does not intimate that these crystals are noxious or hurtful, or that their presence imparts any impure taint to the mass in which they are so plentifully distributed. It, however, is evident that just in proportion to their extent the mass of which they form a component part must be less rich, and correspondingly less nutritious than the butter, which is wholly butter, and nothing else.' The last part of this paragraph is so absurdly ridiculous that I hardly think it requires answering; but, fearing that your readers might accept the same without giving thought to it (as it was undoubtedly written without proper thought or consideration), I think it may be well to answer it, and in the shortest way possible, which I will do by asking a simple question: Is crystallized sugar 'less rich, and correspondingly less nutritious,' than powdered sugar? If you think so, just powder some of the crystals and try it. (Is ice less pure than the water out of which it forms?)

"Figure 7 represents a sample of rancid butter bought on Eleventh Avenue, the retail price being twenty cents a pound. It will be seen on examining this figure that dark, black indentations are to be seen in most of the globules, showing that decomposition is in progress. This decomposition is the first stage of putrifaction, which can only take place by the

growth and development of multitudes of minute organisms. All of the soluble fats which give the aroma
and delicate flavor of butter are, by the growth of the
organisms, decomposed into rancid acids, which, when
taken internally, bring about a general disorder of the
system, producing ' violent cramping and purging, and
often setting up putrefaction in the tissues.' There
can be no doubt that a very large per cent. of the sick-
ness among the poorer classes is due to the use of

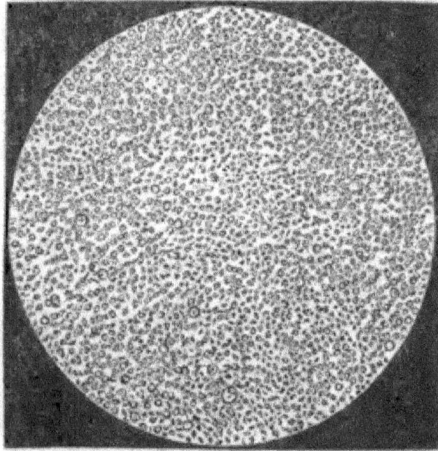

Fig. 7.

rancid butter, who, before the introduction of oleomargarine butter, were compelled to buy it, owing to the
high price of a better article. I say owing to the high
price of a better article: this statement is not altogether
correct; for, if they had the inclination to buy a pure
sweet article, free from rancidity, it would be, under
the present condition of things, an impossibility to
supply their demand. It is the admission of the Secretary of the American Dairymen's Association that
only five per cent. of the 800,000,000 pounds—the an-

nual production of butter—is a perfect article. Mr.
Curtiss, to explain this statement, says the five per
cent. means the 'strictly fancy' butter, and that at
least twenty-five per cent. will be pronounced fine,
while fifty per cent. of the butter is sweet and palatable, and also wholesome.   This explanation, although
somewhat more favorable to dairymen, is certainly not
saying very much.   To think that, by their own admission, 400,000,000 pounds of butter sold in this country

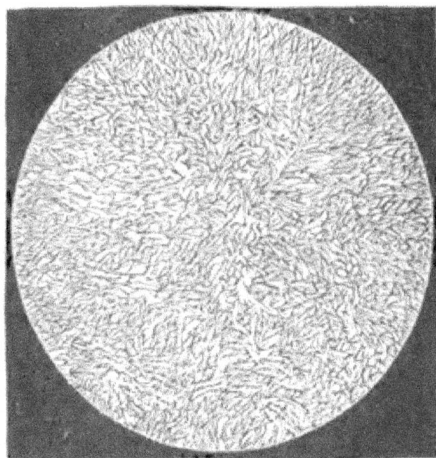

Fig 8.

is offered at a somewhat lower price than the price of
good butter, because it is in a state of decomposition,
tainted by rancid acids and swarming with minute organisms; and because of its cheapness, the poor people
had to purchase it before the introduction of oleomargarine butter!   Does this speak well for the dairymen?
No: it only speaks for the filthiness of the dairy; for
cleanliness is nine-tenths of the secret of making a
pure, sweet butter.   One drop of milk left in the milk-
pail, the milk-pan, or the churn, soon becomes the

proper medium for the growth and development of the numerous germs of life which float in our atmosphere —fermentation and putrefaction of this little drop of milk soon take place. Add now to either of these different apparatuses fresh milk or cream, and that which was fresh and sweet before adding is now tainted, itself in the process of decomposition.

"Figure 8 represents stearine, which will be seen to be in an entirely crystalline condition. The following is the report of Prof. J. W. S. Arnold on the samples examined by him, all of which I carefully examined myself, and can verify the accuracy of his investigation:

"PHYSIOLOGICAL LABORATORY, MEDICAL DEPARTMENT, UNIVERSITY OF NEW YORK, June 17, 1878.

"DR. H. W. MOTT, JR.:

"My Dear Sir—I have made a careful microscopical examination of the samples of caul-fat, stearine, and oleomargarine which you placed in my hands. These substances are entirely free from any impurity or injurious material detectable by the microscope. I have also submitted the oleomargarine butter to a similar examination, comparing it with natural butter, and finding the oleomargarine butter to consist of exceedingly clear and beautiful oil globules, a sufficient proof of its purity. The specimen of rancid butter shows very nicely the granular and irregular oil globules characteristic of decomposing fat. I send you a series of photo-micrographs of the various fats and butter examined. The magnifying power equals a four-tenths objective and 'A' eye-piece.

"Very truly yours,
"J. W. S. ARNOLD, A. M., M. D.

"Further reference to Mr. Michell's article almost seems a waste of time; but, as he makes some sensational remarks about finding in the butter 'parts of the tissue of the animal, with fragments and cells of a suspicious character,' and then in connection with these remarks, speaking of trichinæ, and of diseases which can be communicated from animals to man. Although there is not the least foundation for his imaginary speculations, I think it well to answer a few of the more prominent ones. In the first place, if Mr. Michell understood how to prepare a slide with oleomargarine butter for microscopical examination, he would have obtained results which could not be distinguished from the result obtained when natural butter is examined, as demonstrated by Figures 4 and 5. Then he would not have discovered any tissue and remarkable cells; but,

NOT KNOWING HOW TO EXAMINE A SAMPLE,

he obtained any number of distorted-shaped bodies, which were entirely the result of ignorance or intentional misrepresentation. Again: Michell calls attention to the fact that, as the fat is never submitted to a higher temperature than 120° Fahrenheit, 'it is merely liquefied, and that it would appear to follow the germs of disease (or their equivalent morbid secretions); and embryoes of parasites are thus liable to be transferred in a living condition into the system of those who make use of this substance.'

" The best answer to these remarks is probably a confession which Mr. Michell made to me personally when he stated that, in all his examinations and in all his readings, he had never seen or heard of germs of disease or embryoes of parasites in caul-fat. And still, acquainted with those facts, he was unprincipled enough to insinuate directly to the contrary. I give below a few paragraps from some correspondence which has been carried on respecting this subject by two of the highest authorities in this country on any subject connected with parasites. The first is from a letter by Prof. A. E. Verrill, A. M., S. B. of Yale College.

"In regard to worms in beef fat, I will state definitely that no such instances are known to occur. Nor has trichinæ been observed either in the fat or flesh, except when the embryoes have been purposely fed to the animals before killing them (for experimental purposes).

"The second is from two letters by Prof. William H. Brewer, also of Yale College:

"The idea that oleomargarine is more dangerous than butter, because heated to only 120 degrees Fahrenheit, is simply nonsense.

"Professor Brewer also gave the following written answers to the questions cited below:

"First—Do parasites, that could find their way into the human system through the use of oleomargarine as food, infest the bovine race?
"To this I answer: 'Not that I have ever heard of. If such exist, science has not yet found them. The bovine race, like most other creatures, have parasites, but no species has yet been described which would be transmitted to man in that way.'
"Second—Can the microscope be relied on to distinguish between the butter fats, whether natural or artificial?
"On this I cannot speak with certainty. My belief is that it cannot, so far as the mere fats are concerned; but that it would be an aid to chemistry, in the hands of a skillful expert, to distinguish between butter and other compounds of which such fats are ingredients.
"Third—Is not oleomargarine, as made by the Mége patent, as wholesome and nutritious as cream butter?
"So far as chemistry and common sense suggest, I see no reason why it should not be as wholesome and nutritious as cream butter, and will so believe unless its actual use demonstrates to the contrary.

"THE MICROSCOPE THEN DEMONSTRATES

oleomargarine to be entirely free from 'any impurity or injurious material,' and shows that oleomargarine butter, instead of consisting of 'crystals and tissues of animals, with fragments and cells of a suspicious character,' consists of exceedingly 'clear and beautiful oil globules,' the same as the purest natural butter. Although this investigation has taken a great deal of time, with the assistance of the ablest scientific men in the country to refute the gross misrepresentations of Mr. Michell, it will have two effects: ǒne, to more publicly establish the remarkable purity of oleomargarine butter; and the other to influence the public in the future to hesitate to accept the imaginary results of an ignorant amateur. The microscope, then, establishes the absolute purity of oleomargarine butter. What now can chemical analysis say? The result of a careful qualitative analysis conducted by myself has demonstarted that every constituent found in natural butter is to be found in the artificial products. This being the case, let us turn our attention to quantitative analysis, and see how each constituent compares with each other as to quantity present.

" The following analyses which I have just conducted of natural and artificial butter are the most elaborate which have yet been made:

ANALYSES OF NATURAL AND ARTIFICIAL BUTTER, BY DR. H. A. MOTT, JR.

Constituents.		No. 1. Natural Butter.	No. 2. Artificial Butter.
Water		11,968	11,203
Butter solids		88,032	88,797
		100.000	100.000
Insol. fats	Olein	} 23.824	24.893
	Palmitin		
	Stearine	} 51.422	56.29
	Arachin		
	Myristin		
Sol. fats	Butyrin	} 7.432	1.823
	Caprin		
	Caproin		
	Caprylin		
Casein		.192	.621
Salt		5.162	5.162
Coloring matter		Trace.	Trace.
		88.032	88.797

" No. 1 is calculated to the same percentage of salt as No. 2.

" By examining the above two analyses it will be seen that the artificial butter contains a somewhat larger percentage of butter solids. The percentage of soluble fats which was determined by Herner's new method in artificial butter is somewhat less than in the natural product—quite sufficient, though, to give the product a good flavor and aroma, but hardly sufficient, when decomposed, to render the product rancid; and it is for this reason that oleomargarine butter keeps so much longer than natural butter. Chemical analysis joined with the microscope to prove the identity of natural and artificial butter, and demonstrate the absolute purity of the latter. It is to be hoped, in the face of these facts, especially when the Board of Health pronounces it a pure and wholesome article of food, that all further controversy is at an end forever. It will be so to science, and also to all honest and fair-minded dealers, but not to men whose avarice is paramount to principle. So long as they can realize their five and ten per cent. on the 400,000,000 pounds of impure, rancid butter, just so long will they endeavor to hunt up Michell in every shape and form, having no regard whatever for the health of the great masses of people to whom such impurities are dealt out."

Prof. Morley, of Hudson, Ohio, a distinguished chemist and microscopist, writes:

" I could distinguish no crystal of oleomargarine, and no other substance except fragments of crystals of salt. The microscope shows nothing which should justify any prejudice against oleomargarine butter."

Prof. Thomas Taylor, a microscopist in the Agricultural Department at Washington, after making a thorough investigation of oleomargarine butter manufactured by the American Manufacturing Company of Baltimore, says:

"It is my conviction that oleomargarine butter is destined, at no distant day, to be placed side by side with the best creamery butter, and drive out of the market all inferior grades."

Prof. Peter Collier, chemist of the Agricultural Department at Washington, submitted to Commissioner Le Duc a report of a comparative analysis of oleomargarine and dairy butter. Both he and Prof. Taylor agree in the statement that the artificial butter submitted to analysis shows no marked deviation from ordinary pure butter as found in the market, and there is no evidence of anything injurious or abnormal.

The Board of Health of New York, of which Prof. C. F. Chandler is president, having been requested by the New York State Senate to investigate oleomargarine butter as to its purity and wholesomeness, reported

"THAT OLEOMARGARINE IS A GOOD AND WHOLESOME ARTICLE OF FOOD."

Yet it is on such authority as Michell's, a man of no scientific attainments or pursuits, that G. T. Angell made such statements before the Association at Saratoga. Evidently he must have been ignorant of the standing and attainments of the author from whom he was quoting. If the investigations of amateurs such as Michell are to have weight and bearing against the testimony of such an array of known scientists, then science is turned into ridicule.

We are led to ask, Why this opposition to an industry in the face of such cumulative and undoubted testimony as to its merits? Either oleomargarine butter is a meritorious article of commerce, or it is a base fraud. If there is any reliance to be placed on testimony at all, and if we are to judge from evidence, it is clearly a settled fact that it is found to be an eminently wholesome product. Hyppolite Mége, of Paris, France, who brought to light this law of nature—that the fat of cattle is the origin and only source of butter—on this discovery alone, aside from his other efforts in behalf of science, established his position as one of the first chemists in the world.

We are not surprised that the ordinary mind cannot grasp and understand

SO GRAND A DISCOVERY,

which is in direct conflict with the recognized method of making butter. But what shall be said of merchants who deal in this article, and whose avarice would prompt them to combat the manufacture of an article which must prove so beneficial to the people. X It is now an assured success, and is driving out of market a large proportion of ordinary butter. The *London Grocer* of January 5, 1878, the greatest of commercial papers, calls it the butter of the future, and recommends its use in the strongest terms. The authorities given prove that it goes farther as an article of food, and remains pure and sweet much longer, than ordinary butter, which keeps but a few days in a warm climate before rancidity and decomposition take place. Prof. Arnold, Secretary of the American Dairy Association, in his annual report, makes the remarkable statement that out of 800,000,000 of pounds, the annual production in this country, but five per cent. is a perfect article of food. But what becomes of the unwholesome ninety-five per cent.? It is this vast aggregate of impure food that oleomargarine is driving out of the markets. Its opponents admit that for the year 1878, 90,000,000 pounds of this product was consumed in this country alone, while a larger amount was exported to Germany, France, and Holland, where it was churned into butter, and thence transported to England. It is stated, in a foreign commercial journal of March 1, 1878, that two butter-making firms of Holland exported weekly to the United Kingdom an amount representing £25,000, or $125,000, including both natural and artificial butter. For the manufacture of artificial butter these two firms use daily 20,000 kilogrammes of oleomargarine, and 8,000 liters of new milk. This industry bears, in a most important manner,

UPON THE CATTLE INTERESTS

of this country. Within the past few years an enormous demand has been created abroad for canned meat, fresh beef, and live cattle. Hundreds of thousands are annually required to meet this want. One company, the East St. Louis Canning Company, slaughters daily 700 head of cattle, or about 2,500,000 during the year, and exports the greater portion in the shape of canned meats. The result is that beef in our market commands a much higher price in proportion than other articles of food. To produce a larger supply is a problem of easy solution to the farmers. Let them cease to slaughter millions of calves annually before they are fit for food, and raise them on the milk from which butter has been taken.

If the old method of producing butter cannot maintain itself without misrepresentations and special State enactments, then it should and will disappear, and give place to the new product, by which the people are furnished a pure and wholesome butter. If the bitter and unjust opposition waged against this industry had been brought to bear against all new labor-saving methods, then long since we should have cast aside the reaper and gone back to the sickle. In like manner the mower would have been replaced by the scythe. Such opposition invites us to follow a blind prejudice which seeks to destroy every innovation; but the world moves, and old methods are being daily forced to recognize the merits of the new. Therefore, the manufacture of oleomargarine butter should be gladly welcomed as an important and valuable industry, believing that it will meet a great want by furnishing a pure and wholesome butter.

INDORSEMENT OF OLEMARGARINE

BY THE

PRODUCE EXCHANGE.

WHEREAS, The manufacture of oleomargarine and oleomargarine butter, or butterine, has been indorsed by men eminent in science, as the following certificates show;

Therefore, we, members of the New York Produce Exchange, hereby recognize the said product as a pure and wholesome article of food, and of value to commerce.

NAMES.	ADDRESS.
John Anderson,	7 Bowling Green.
James Thallon,	17 Moore St.
Fowler Bros.,	17 Broadway.
Thomas & Co.,	5 Bowling Green.
Wm. Miller,	13 Moore St.
Alex. D. Corson,	13 Moore St.
Cecil Rowson,	35 Broadway.
John M. & Henry Webb,	5 Bowling Green.
Osborn Bros.,	5 Bowling Green.
F. Kiorboe,	5 Bowling Green.
David Muir,	2 Broadway.
John Orpe,	3 Broadway.
John G. Dale,	31 and 33 Broadway.
E. T. Hopkins,	3 Bowling Green.
A. H. Turner,	12 Bridge St.
Thos. D. Harrison,	27 Water St.
H. K. & F. B. Thurber & Co.,	West Broadway and Reade.
C. F. Emerson & Co.,	31 Water St.
John Cahill,	42 Whitehall St.
Peter Jones,	1 Water St.
G. H. Crichton,	30 Whitehall St.
Knapp & Co.,	111 Broad St.
C. H. Johnson,	27 Front St.
Fred Stephenson,	31 Front St.
Gould H. Thorp & Co.,	109 Broad St.
E. A. Johnson,	109 Broad St.

3

NAMES.	ADDRESS.
Theo. Perry,	15 Water.
John F. Levers,	31 Water St.
John A. Sullivan,	13 Whitehall St.
Theophilus M. Marc,	43 Exchange Place.
Thomas Whitman,	13 Whitehall St.
Geo. McGrath,	12 Front St.
V. W. McFarlane,	19 South William St.
G. M. Merrielees,	Exchange Building.
W. E. Adams,	17 Moore St.
James B. Bouck,	111 Broad St.
J. W. Follett,	38 Whitehall St.
C. W. Strachan,	82 Broad St.
C. H. Cadwell,	115 Broad St.
Auguste Vatable,	82 Beaver St.
Geo. H. Webster,	129 Broad St.
H. P. Low,	31 Water St.
John H. Emanuel,	131 Pearl St.
John Goggin,	38 Whitehall St.
Geo. F. Patrick,	37 Whitehall St.
Peter Brett,	37 Whitehall St.
William H. Fox,	20 Platt St.
Alfred Churchman,	17 Moore St.
Jno. A. Cooper,	9 Water St.
Chas. D. Sabin,	25 Water St.
Goulard, Rouse & Bostwick,	36 Whitehall St.
G. F. Bechtel, Jr.,	109 Water St.
F. A. Lowe,	31 Water St.
C. E. Cole,	41 Broad St.
E. Mathews,	65 Beaver St.
Wm. P. Bensel,	350 Washington St.
E. A. Wallis,	67 Pearl St.
Edward Read,	115 Broad St.
Christ. F. Tietjen,	1 Leonard St.
O. H. Blackman,	200 Forsyth St.
E. B. Terrill,	72 Beaver St.
Asa Stevens,	86 Broad St.
Jas. Edmiston,	70 Beaver St.
Thos. I. McGrath,	172 Reade St.
S. Van Brunt,	59 Beaver St.
J. A. Sperry,	New Haven.
L. J. Rice,	28 Moore St.
M. S. Popham,	80 Broad St.
W. S. Cobb,	499 Washington St.
Jos. S. Thayer,	129 Broad St.
R. F. Martin,	129 Broad St.
Geo. C. Stedge,	115 Broad St.
C. B. Lathrop,	122 Broad St.
Chas. A. Smith,	115 Broad St.
W. S. Bracken,	52 Exchange Place.

NAMES.	ADDRESS.
Chas. Spear,	85 West St.
A. Sinclair,	14 Moore St.
Robert R. Phillips,	64 Beaver St.
F. W. Cummuskey,	58 Greenwich St.
Geo. N. Carhart,	19 Broadway.
J. W. Alt,	3 State St.
Thos. E. Cole,	35 Broad St.
E. S. Whitman,	159 Front St.
Benj. Hicks,	165 Broad St.
Rob't S. Fish,	60 Beaver St.
Archibald Harris,	189 and 191 Front St.
C. Medcafe,	39 Pearl St.
Thomas Martin,	189 Front St.
F. Fortman,	27 South William St.
H. G. M. Linton,	33 Nassau St.
I. & C. Moore & Co.,	142 Pearl St.
E. T. Barrows,	60 Beaver St.
J. C. Gale,	Pier 30, North River.
Archibald Baxter,	17 Broadway.
Bechstein & Co.	100 Hudson St.
W. H. McNeil,	641 West 38th St.
H. J. Hayne,	160 Front St.
Thos. Rafferty,	44th St. and E. River.
S. F. Havens,	115 Broad St.
Wm. Hardy,	51 Pearl St.
Wm. Williamson,	63 Pearl St.
G. Speckel,	44 Beaver St.
Jos. Lockitt,	184 Fulton St., Brooklyn.
G. Perry,	19 Old Slip.
Frederick W. Phillips,	31 Moore St.
Samuel Goodhue,	13 Water St.
L. G. Biglow,	35 Broadway.
W. C. Smith & Co.,	53 Exchange Place.
Henry Dillon,	29 Front St.
Levi G. Burgess,	66 South St.
F. A. Van Idenstine,	272 Hudson St., Brooklyn.
Edward H. Bunker,	64 Beaver St.
Henry C. Frink,	30 Broadway.
C. W. Biglow,	40 Broadway.
Chas. W. Kurtz,	25 Pearl St.
F. W. Kriege,	5 William St.
J. Hess,	17 South William St.
Snow & Burgess,	60 South St.
C. D. Georgiades,	Produce Exchange.
J. B. Smull,	31 and 33 Broadway.
R. Parkinson,	40 Whitehall St.
F. P. Albert,	13 Moore St.
P. M. Millspaugh,	16 Broadway.
C. A. Kimball,	127 Water St.

NAMES.	ADDRESS.
C. D. Moulton,	40 Broadway.
Stephen Whitman,	99 Pearl St.
F. X. Schedler,	32 Pearl St.
M. Groh.	80 Beaver St.
D. K. Baker,	335 Greenwich St.
E. W. Mascord,	2 State St.
R. H. Hazeltine,	31 Pearl St.
E. R. Livermore,	119 Broad St.
R. W. Kennedy,	145 Reade St.
J. A. Chamberlain,	25 Pearl St.
Lockitt & Co., Packers,	Brooklyn.
Chamberlain, Roe & Co.,	25 Pearl St.
W. Cockle,	124 Front St.
A. A. Jones,	111 Broad St.
Thos. C. Dow,	Exchange Place.
A. D. Sterlin,	1 Moore St.
E. B. Pearsall,	46 Front St.
E. G. Burgess,	35 Pearl St.
C. B. Hancock,	2 Broadway.
W. H. Story,	2 Broadway.
Henry B. Hebert,	14 Moore St.
Ira Olds & Co.,	17 Broadway.
S. B. Joseph,	13 Moore St.
J. E. Jenkins.	61 Beaver St.
Paul Worth,	18 William St.
H. L. Daniels,	18 William St.
E. S. Herrick,	11 State St.
E. Munn,	61 Beaver St.
A. S. Jewell,	27 Water St.
A. R. Gray,	110 Broad St.
Wm. M. Deverall,	134 Pearl St.
Lillienthal Bros. & Stern,	Cedar St.
F. L. Whittemore,	4 State St.
E. H. Walker,	38 Whitehall St.
G. H. Roberts,	3 Front St.
H. C. Hicks,	71 Broadway.
F. D. Winchester,	38 Whitehall St.
E. Ibbotson,	69 Broadway.
C. H. Blanchard,	6 Bowling Green.
P. Westervelt,	19 Broadway.
C. N. Sheppard,	5 Bowling Green
Jno. J. Ferris,	37 Pearl St.
E. C. Beile,	43 Exchange Place.
W. Eismann,	150 Broome St.
S. W. Hoyt,	Hudson & Duane Sts.
H. Sabin,	25 Water.

And many others.

OLEOMARGARINE BUTTER.

Answer of Prof. Chandler to a Congressional Inquiry.

Hon. Morgan R. Wise of Pennsylvania, Chairman of the Committee on Manufactures of the House of Representatives, addressed a letter to Prof. Charles F. Chandler, President of the New York Board of Health, informing him that the Committee has under consideration a bill in relation to adulterations in food and drink, and asking whether the article known as oleomargarine, or butterine, is wholesome or unwholesome, and for such other information as might be in the possession of the Board. The following is Prof. Chandler's response:

HEALTH DEPARTMENT, 301 MOTT STREET,
NEW YORK, March 27, 1880.

MY DEAR SIR:

In reply to your letter of inquiry, I would say that I have been familiar with the discovery of Mége Mauries, and its application in the manufacture of artificial butter, called "butterine," or "oleomargarine," since the date of its first publication.

I have frequently seen it manufactured, witnessing all the operations, and examining both the material and the product.

I have studied the subject with special reference to

the question of its use as food, in comparison with the ordinary butter made from cream, and have satisfied myself that it is quite as valuable as the butter from the cow; that the material from which it is manufactured is perfectly fresh beef suet; that the processes are harmless; that the manufacture is conducted with great cleanliness. The product is palatable and wholesome, and I regard it as a most valuable article of food, and consider the discovery of Mége Mauries as marking an era in the chemistry of the fats.

Butterine is manufactured of uniform quality the year round, and can be sold at a price far below that at which ordinary butter is sold. It does not readily become rancid, and is free from the objectionable taste and odor which characterize a large proportion of the butter sold in this market.

I am informed that there are at present thirteen factories in the United States licensed under the patents to manufacture this butter. The Commercial Manufacturing Company of New York is making at the present from 30,000 to 40,000 lbs. daily. In addition to this industry, there is a large manufacture of what is known as "oleomargarine oil," which is shipped as such to Europe, to be there converted into butter; so that this product has become an important article of export to foreign countries.

The beef suet which was formerly converted into common tallow, only suitable for the manufacture of soap, is, by this beautiful discovery, now manufactured into oleomargarine oil and stearine, of double the value of the tallow formerly produced. The following analyses, made by Drs. Brown and Mott, sufficiently illustrate the composition of the butterine:

Constituents.	No. 1. Natural Butter.	No. 2. Artificial Butter.
Water	11.968	11.203
Butter solids	88.032	88.797
	100.000	100.000
Insol. fats { Olein, Palmatin, Stearine, Arachin, Myristin }	23.824, 51.422	24.893, 56.29
Sol. fats { Butyrin, Caprin, Caproin, Caprylin }	7.432	1.823
Casein	.192	.621
Salt	5.162	5.162
Coloring matter	Trace.	Trace.
	88.032	88.797

Last winter a resolution was adopted by the Legislature of the State of New York, requesting the Board of Health of the city of New York to investigate the subject, and report whether, in its opinion, the butterine is a wholesome article of food. In response to this resolution, the Board of Health stated that in its opinion there is no sanitary objection whatever to the unrestricted manufacture and sale of this substance.

In support of my opinion herein expressed, I inclose the statement to the same effect made by Prof. George F. Barker, of the University of Pennsylvania; Dr. Henry A. Mott, Jr., of New York; Prof. S. C. Caldwell, of Cornell University; Prof. S. W. Johnson, of Yale College; Prof. C. A. Goessmann, of the Massachusetts Agricultural College; Prof. Henry Morton, of the Stevens Institute of Technology of Hoboken; Dr. Chas. P. Williams of Philadelphia; Prof. W. O. Atwater, of the Wesleyan University at Middletown, Conn.; and

6

Prof. J. W. S. Arnold, of the Medical Department of the University of New York.

Hoping that this my reply contains all the information you desire, I remain,

Very respectfully yours,
CH. F. CHANDLER, Ph. D.,
Prest. of the Board of Health.

To Hon. M. R. Wise,
Chairman of the Committee on Manufactures,
House of Representatives, Washington, D. C.

[*Letter from Prof. Barker.*]

University of Pennsylvania,
Philadelphia, March 22, 1880.

The United States Dairy Co.

Gentlemen: In reply to your inquiry, I would say that I have been acquainted for several years with the discovery of Mége Mauries for producing butterine from oleomargarine fat. In theory, the process should yield a product resembling butter in all essential respects, having identically the same fatty constituents. The butterine prepared under the inventor's patents is, therefore, in my opinion, quite as valuable a nutritive agent as butter itself. In practice, the process of manufacture, as I have witnessed it, is conducted with care and great cleanliness. The butterine produced is pure and of excellent quality, is perfectly wholesome, and is desirable as an article of food. I can see no reason why butterine should not be an entirely satisfactory equivalent for ordinary butter, whether considered from the physiological or commercial standpoint.

Respectfully yours,
GEORGE F. BARKER.

[*Letter from Prof. Morton.*]

Stevens Institute of Technology,
Hoboken, New Jersey, March 16, 1880.

United States Dairy Co.

Gentleman: During the last three years I have had occasion to examine the product known as artificial butter, oleomargarine, or butterine, first produced by M. Mége, of Paris, and described by him in his patent of July 17, 1869.

I have also frequently witnessed the manufacture of this material, and with these opportunities of knowing exactly what it is, I am able to say with confidence that it contains nothing whatever which is injurious as an article of diet; but, on the contrary, is essentially identical with the best fresh butter, and is very superior to much of the butter made from cream alone which is found in the market.

The conditions of its manufacture involve a degree of cleanliness and consequent purity in the product such as are by no means necessarily or generally attained in the ordinary making of butter from cream. Yours, etc.,

HENRY MORTON.

———

[*Letter from Prof. Johnson.*]

SHEFFIELD SCIENTIFIC SCHOOL OF YALE COLLEGE, NEW HAVEN, CONNECTICUT, March 20, 1880.

THE UNITED STATES DAIRY CO.

Gentlemen: I am acquainted with the process discovered by M. Mége for producing the article known in commerce as oleomargarine, or butterine.

I have witnessed the manufacture in all its stages, as carried out on the large scale, and I can assert that when it is conducted according to the specifications of M. Mége, it cannot fail to yield a product that is entirely attractive and wholesome as food, and one that is for all ordinary culinary and nutritive purposes the full equivalent of good butter made from cream.

Oleomargarine butter has the closest resemblance to butter made from cream in its external qualities—color, flavor, and texture. It has the same appearance under the microscope, and in chemical composition differs not in the nature, but only in the proportions of its components. It is therefore fair to pronounce them essentially identical.

While oleomargarine contains less of those flavoring principles which characterize the choicest butter, it is, perhaps, for that very reason, comparatively free from the tendency to change and taint which speedily renders a large proportion of butter unfit for human food.

I regard the manufacture of oleomargarine or butterine as a legitimate and beneficent industry.

S. W. JOHNSON,

Professor of Theoretical and Agricultural Chemistry; Director of the Connecticut Agricultural Experiment Station.

[Letter from Prof. Caldwell.]

CHEMICAL LABRATORY, CORNELL UNIVERSITY,
ITHACA, N. Y., March 20, 1880.

I have witnessed, in all its stages, the manufacture of " oleomargarine " and of oleomargarine butter, or " butterine."

The process for oleomargarine when properly conducted, as in the works of the Commercial Manufacturing Co., is cleanly throughout, and includes every reasonable precaution necessary to secure a product entirely free from animal tissue, or any other impurity, and which shall consist of pure fat made up of the fats commonly known as oleine and margarine. It is, when thus prepared, a tasteless and inodorous substance, possessing no qualities whatever that can make it in the least degree unwholesome, when used in reasonable quantities, as an article of food.

In the manufacture of butterine, since nothing but milk, annotto, and salt, together with perhaps a little water from clean ice, are added to this oleomargarine, to be intimately mixed with it by churning and other operations, I have no hesitation in affirming that this also, when properly made according to the Mége patent and other patents held by the United States Dairy Co., and when used in reasonable quantities, is a perfectly wholesome article of food ; and that, while not equal to fine butter in respect to flavor, it nevertheless contains all the essential ingredients of butter; and since it contains a smaller proportion of volatile fats than is found in genuine butter, it is, in my opinion, less liable to become rancid.

It cannot enter into competition with fine butter ; but in so far as it may serve to drive poor butter out of the market, its manufacture will be a public benefit.   S. C. CALDWELL.

[Letter from Prof. Goessmann.]

AMHERST, MASS., March 20, 1880.

UNITED STATES DAIRY CO., NEW YORK.

Gentlemen: I have visited, on the 17th and 18th of the present month, your factory on West Forty-eighth Street, for the purpose of studying your mode of applying Mége's discovery for the manufacture of oleomargarine butter, or butterine. A careful examination into the character of the material turned to account, as well as into the details of the entire management of the manufacturing operation, has convinced me that your product is made with care, and furnishes thus a wholesome article of food. Your oleomargarine butter, or butterine, compares in general appearance and in taste very favorably with the average quality of the better kinds of the dairy butter in our markets. In its composition it resembles that of the ordinary dairy butter; and in its keeping quality, under corresponding circumstances, I believe it will surpass the former; for it contains a smaller percentage of those constituents (glycerides of volatile acids) which, in the main, cause the well-known rancid taste and odor of a stored butter.

I am, very respectfully yours,

C. A. GOESSMANN, Ph. D.,

Professor of Chemistry.

———

[*Letter from Dr. Williams.*]

LABORATORY, No. 912 SAMSON STREET,
PHILADELPHIA, March 22, 1880.

During a period of upwards of two years I have been practically familiar with the details of the manufacture by the Mége method of oleomargarine butter, or "butterine." From my experience and observation of the care and cleanliness absolutely necessary in the manufacture of this product, together with my knowledge of its composition, I am satisfied that it is a pure and wholesome article of food, and in this respect, as well as in respect to its chemical composition, fully the equivalent of the best quality of dairy butter.

I will add further, that, owing to the presence of a less quantity of the volatile fats, the keeping qualities of the oleomargarine butter are far superior to those of the dairy product.

CHARLES P. WILLIAMS, Ph. D.,

Analytical Chemist; late Director and Professor Missouri School of Mines, State University.

———

[*Letter from Dr. Mott.*]

H. A. MOTT, JR., Ph. D., E. M.,
ANALYTICAL AND CONSULTING CHEMIST,
OFFICE, 117 WALL STREET,
NEW YORK, March 12, 1880.

UNITED STATES DAIRY CO.

Gentlemen: Having been acquainted for the past six years with the process of the manufacture of the product called oleomargarine butter, or butterine, and having made numerous microscopical and chemical examinations of the product, I am clearly of the opinion that the product called oleomargarine butter is essentially identical with butter made from cream ; and as the former contains less of those fats which, when decomposed, render the product rancid, it can be kept pure and sweet for a much longer time.

I consider the product of the Mége discovery a perfectly pure and wholesome article of food, which is destined to supplant the inferior grades of butter, and be placed side by side with the best products of the creamery.

Respectfully,
HENRY A. MOTT, Jr., Ph. D.

————

[*Letter from Prof. Arnold.*]

UNIVERSITY PHYSIOLOGICAL LABORATORY,
410 EAST 26TH ST., April 2, 1880.

This is to certify that I have carefully examined the "Mége Patent Process" for the manufacture of oleomargarine butter, or butterine ; that I have seen and tasted at the factory each and every ingredient employed ; that I have made thorough microscopical examinations of the materials used and of the butter ; and I consider that each and every article employed in the manufacture of oleomargarine butter, or butterine, is perfectly pure and wholesome ; that the oleomargarine butter differs in no essential manner from butter made from cream ; in fact, the oleomargarine butter possesses the advantage over natural butter of not decomposing so readily, as it contains fewer volatile fats. In my opinion, oleomargarine is to be considered a great discovery, a blessing for the poor, and in every way a perfectly pure, wholesome, and palatable article of food.

J. W. S. ARNOLD, A.M., M.D.
Prof. Physiology and Histology, Med. Dep. Univ. New York.

————

[*Letter from Prof. Atwater.*]

WESLEYAN UNIVERSITY,
MIDDLETOWN, CONN., March 29, 1880.

I have carefully looked into the theory and the practice of the manufacture of butterine (oleomargarine) by the "Mége process," and examined the product. A consideration of the materials used, the process of manufacture, and the chemical and microscopical character of the butterine, seem to me to fully justify the following statements:

As to its qualitative composition, it contains essentially the same ingredients as natural butter from cows' milk.

Quantitatively, it differs from ordinary butter in having but little of the volatile fats which, while they are agreeable in flavor, are, at the same time, liable to rancidity. I should, accordingly, expect butterine to keep better than ordinary butter. The best evidence within my reach indicates that just such is the case. The butterine is perfectly wholesome and healthy, and has a high nutritious value. The same entirely favorable opinion I find expressed by the most prominent European authorities—English, French, and German— who are unanimous in their high estimate of the value of the "Mége discovery," and approval of the material whose production has there-by been made practicable.

I am, very truly yours,

W. O. ATWATER.

Award of the American Institute.

OFFICE OF THE GENERAL SUPERINTENDENT OF THE AMERICAN INSTITUTE OF THE CITY OF NEW YORK, NEW YORK, March 24, 1880.

Copy of the Judges' Report in Department VII., Group 3, at the Forty-seventh Exhibition of the American Institute, held in the City of New York, October and November, 1878.

No. 879.—OLEOMARGARINE BUTTER.

COMMERCIAL MANUFACTURING CO.,
643 WEST 48TH STREET, NEW YORK.

The oleomargarine butter (Mége's process) has the general appearance of the usual style of good dairy butter. The texture presents some slight difference to the eye of an expert. The absence of some of the elements which give the peculiar aroma to the best quality of spring-grass butter tends to prevent the approach of any unpleasant change in this article, and it is thus enabled to resist the effects of time, as upon a long sea voyage.

We have examined the process of manufacture, and find the product clean and wholesome.

While the best quality of dairy butter must still maintain its superiority, any departure from the most perfect manufacture will make the oleomargarine a dangerous rival.

The process utilizes valuable animal products, and makes useful in the kitchen and upon the dining-table much that was formerly used for less important purposes; and for this and its keeping qualities it should receive some recognition by the Institute.

A. S. HEATH, M.D.,
ROBERT J. DODGE, } *Judges.*
WILLET SEAMAN,

The Medal of Excellence Awarded.

A true copy of the report on file.

D. R. GARDEN,

Assistant Clerk.